CIVICS

KINGFISHER
LONDON & NEW YORK

KINGFISHER
LONDON & NEW YORK

Text and design copyright © Toucan Books Ltd. 2020
Illustrations copyright © Simon Basher 2020
www.basherscience.com

First published 2020 in the United States by Kingfisher
120 Broadway, New York, NY 10271
Kingfisher is an imprint of Macmillan Children's Books, London
All rights reserved.

Author: Shannon Weber
Consultant: Mert Martens
Editor: Anna Southgate
Designer: Dave Jones
Indexer: Marie Lorimer
Proofreader: Mary Budzik

Dedicated to Noel, Natalia, Agi, and Art

Distributed in the U.S. and Canada by Macmillan,
120 Broadway, New York, NY 10271

Library of Congress Cataloging-in-Publication Data has been applied for.

ISBN: 978-0-7534-7627-7 (Hardcover)
ISBN: 978-0-7534-7626-0 (Paperback)

Kingfisher books are available for special promotions and premiums.
For details contact: Special Markets Department, Macmillan, 120 Broadway,
New York, NY 10271

For more information, please visit www.kingfisherbooks.com

Printed in China
9 8 7 6 5 4 3 2 1
1TR/0420/WKT/UG/128MA

CONTENTS

Introduction
Civics

We live in a democracy, a political system dreamed up by the ancient Greeks more than 1500 years ago. *Democracy* means "rule by the common people." It's where citizens of a country, not a king or queen, control the political decisions impacting their lives. In ancient Greece, democracy was "direct," which means all citizens voted on every daily issue. American democracy is a little different and is labeled "representative." Here, a smaller number of people are elected with the idea they'll represent their constituents when they vote on legislation.

This tour of the American government starts with the Constitutional Crew—a bunch of feisty characters who represent the foundation of U.S. government in the 1700s. You'll also meet the Law Makers, the Decision Makers, and the Courtroom Crowd, all colorful personalities from the three branches of government. Together with the Good Citizens, they'll explain all you need to know about civics, and will show you how everyday Americans have fought (and continue to fight) to make society better.

Democracy

Chapter 1
Constitutional Crew

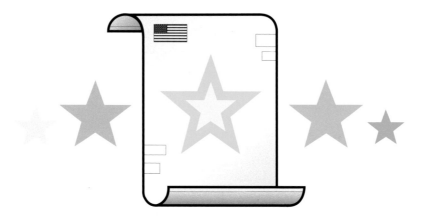

Follow us as we introduce you to the foundation characters of American government. First you'll meet Declaration of Independence, who had the bravery to break away from the control of King George III of England—a move so bold, it resulted in a war! The Constitution gave us the framework for how our new government should work, and Bill of Rights protects many of our basic freedoms. Separation of Powers and Checks and Balances work overtime to make sure the government branches have equal power, while Amendment makes all-important alterations to the Constitution.

Declaration of Independence

The Constitution

Separation of Powers

Checks and Balances

Bill of Rights

Amendment

Separation of Church and State

Popular Sovereignty

Democracy

Electoral College

Declaration of Independence

- Document asserting the people's right to govern themselves
- Addressed to King George III of Great Britain
- Approved by the Second Continental Congress (July 4, 1776)

When the colonists sought independence from British rule, I'm the one who declared "all men are created equal" and are endowed with the "unalienable rights" of life, liberty, and the pursuit of happiness. Should any form of government get in the way of these rights, I said, "it is the right of the people to alter or abolish it, and to institute new government." Bold words indeed!

The colonists were tired of being ruled by a monarch on a faraway continent. With no voice in parliament, they had rebelled against unfair taxes and paying for British troops to keep order. While they engaged in a revolutionary war, I listed their reasons for wanting to leave the British Empire.

- President of the Congress John Hancock was the first to sign the document
- Number of known surviving copies of the Declaration: 26
- The Declaration and Constitution were kept hidden during World War II

Declaration of Independence

The Constitution
Constitutional Crew

* U.S. democracy is based on the Constitution
* Balance is key—government has power, but so do citizens
* Amendments alter articles to the Constitution

Not to brag, but I'm the star of this American government show. I set out the road map for American democracy: how the government is set up, how it operates, what its limits are, and which freedoms are protected. I strike a balance between giving the branches of government authority and protecting citizens from abuses of power.

I date from 1787, when 55 men worked together to improve my predecessor, known as the Articles of Confederation. My opening words are "We the People." They emphasize how the power of government comes from the will of everyday citizens. Since my creation, many groups treated unfairly in society have fought to be included so that they are better protected. My friend Amendment will tell you all about it.

● The oldest and shortest written constitution in the world
● Written in what's now Independence Hall, in Philadelphia, PA
● A five-person "Committee of Style" wrote the final version

The Constitution

Separation of Powers

■ Constitutional Crew

✳ The U.S. government consists of three branches
✳ The branches are legislative, executive, and judicial
✳ Each branch has its own duties and operates independently

A true friend of democracy, I make sure the three branches of government have very specific powers, and that no one branch can dominate over another. I work closely with my friends Checks and Balances.

The three branches of government work like this: the U.S. president has executive power; Congress must stick to its legislative power; and the courts are limited to exercising their judicial power. It means they all have to work together to get things done. My system differs from other types of world governments, such as authoritarianism, where one leader controls the whole show. I'm not greedy, and I make sure nobody else is!

● Legislative branch: makes the laws
● Executive branch: enforces and executes the laws
● Judicial branch: rules on the legality of laws and decides if they are broken

Separation of Powers

Checks and Balances

■ Constitutional Crew

✳ Checks and balances help democracy function
✳ Ensure the three branches of government operate equally
✳ Can stop any one branch from grabbing too much power

You've heard what Separation of Powers has to say about the three branches of government having their own specific powers? We are here to make sure things stay that way! Each branch has ways of "checking" the other two, to stop a corrupt president, Congress, or Supreme Court from taking complete control.

Here's how we work. A president's veto of congressional legislation is an *executive* check on the legislative branch. The power for two-thirds of Congress to override a president's veto is a *legislative* check on the executive branch. And the power of the courts to review laws passed by Congress is a *judicial* check on the legislative branch.

● This concept developed from the idea of separation of powers
● President George Washington issued the first veto on April 5, 1792
● "All men having power ought to be mistrusted."—James Madison

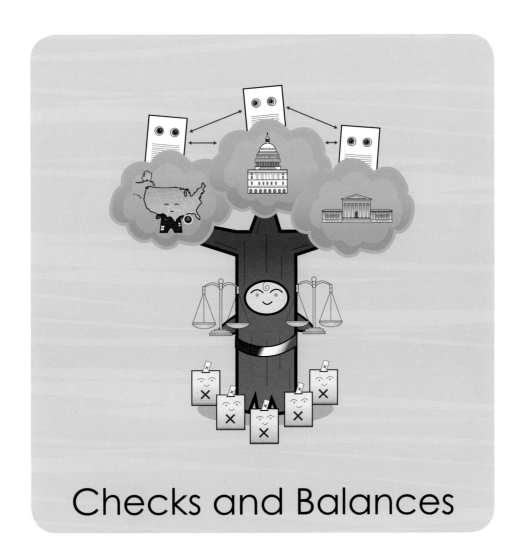

Checks and Balances

Bill of Rights
Constitutional Crew

* The first ten amendments to the Constitution
* Ensured liberties not previously granted by the British king
* Protected the natural rights of the individual

Look at me, standing up for freedom! As the first ten amendments to the Constitution, I specify rights that didn't feature in the original founding document. I include some of the most basic freedoms in American society: freedom of speech and the press, the right to assemble and protest, freedom of religion, and the right to a fair trial.

According to Thomas Jefferson, "[A] bill of rights is what the people are entitled to against every government on earth." James Madison wrote me in 1789, after 9 of the 13 original colonies refused to approve the Constitution. They said it failed to guarantee enough freedom. Madison presented me to the First Congress in 1789, and, bingo, in 1791 the Constitution was approved!

● Elbridge Gerry of gerrymandering fame made the motion to include the bill
● It took 203 years for the 27th Amendment to be ratified (first proposed in 1789)
● Of the 17 amendments proposed, only 10 were included in the final bill

Bill of Rights

17

Amendment

■ Constitutional Crew

✳ An update to the Constitution
✳ Many amendments have sought to eliminate inequality
✳ With high standards for being ratified, these are pretty rare

America has changed since the Constitution was first written. Because of this, it is occasionally updated to live up to its promise of serving "We the People." That's where I come in—in fact, there are 27 of us!

It's hard work becoming an amendment. Two-thirds of Congress or state legislatures must agree even to introduce us. To be "ratified" (passed), 38 out of 50 states (three-fourths) must agree! You've met Bill of Rights— that's the first 10 of us, right there. Many of us arise from the protests of people seeking better treatment. The 13th Amendment abolished slavery after enslaved people and abolitionists fought against it for many generations. The 19th Amendment gave women the right to vote in 1920. Women had been asking for this right since1848!

● More than 11,000 amendments have been proposed in Congress
● The 22nd Amendment stops presidents from serving more than two terms
● The 26th Amendment lowered the voting age from 21 to 18

Amendment

Separation of Church and State

✳ Discussed in the Establishment Clause of the 1st Amendment
✳ Allows people to follow their own personal religious beliefs
✳ Helps protect people who practice minority religions

The chillest defender of personal liberties, I'm all about people practicing whatever religion they want—or no religion at all—without government interference. In a letter of 1802, Thomas Jefferson described me as "a wall of separation between Church & State."

Many European settlers of the 13 colonies came from countries whose subjects had to follow the same branch of Christianity as their monarchs. Some bloody wars were fought as a result. In order to avoid this happening in America, the framers of the Constitution made their new government neutral about faith so that no one can be forced to practice a particular religion.

● Roger Williams founded Rhode Island as a haven of religious freedom
● Thomas Jefferson and Benjamin Franklin practiced Deism
● A theocracy is a system in which a religion determines laws

Separation of
Church and State

Popular Sovereignty
Constitutional Crew

✳ A key theme of the U.S. Constitution
✳ Asserts that government's power lies in its people
✳ This concept has been abused in America's past

I challenge the idea that political power resides in one leader. Instead, I say the people should determine what kind of government they have. My intention is noble, but it can be taken too far. For example, when white people enslaved black people, many argued that each state should decide whether or not to continue slavery. This stance led to the Civil War.

Popular Sovereignty

● French King Louis XVI claimed his power came from God
● The "popular" in popular sovereignty means benefitting the people
● Popular sovereignty excludes the rights of those who cannot vote

Democracy
Constitutional Crew

- The U.S. political system is called a representative democracy
- Elected officials represent "the people" in government
- Officials are elected by their local community

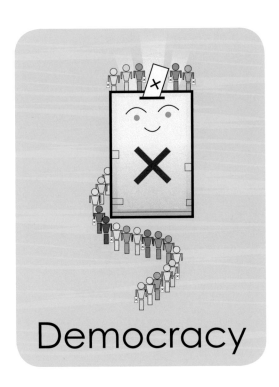

Democracy

There are many types of democracy. In a direct democracy, citizens vote on all matters. In a representative democracy, such as the U.S., people elect officials to run government for them: local mayors, Congress, and the president, for example. I'm helpful in a country as big as the U.S., but some people think direct democracy is better.

- Most Western countries are representative democracies
- Examples of a direct democracy: ancient Greece; modern-day Switzerland
- A country that has no monarch, but elects representatives, is called a republic

Electoral College
■ Constitutional Crew

✳ Sets out the way in which a president is elected
✳ Electors are allocated to each state based on population
✳ Although it sounds like a school, its members rarely meet

As old as the Constitution itself, I arose as a compromise between the Founding Fathers. Some of them wanted *government* to elect the president, while others felt the *people* should do it. In me, they found a middle way. Let me explain the basics.

When Americans vote in a presidential election, they're voting for delegates called "electors." After the election, these electors meet up and (mostly) vote for whichever candidate won in their state. A candidate then needs 270 "electoral" votes to become president. But the electors don't *always* vote for the candidate with the most popular votes, and sometimes another candidate wins instead. Some citizens think my methods are unfair, and would like to see me eliminated by a constitutional amendment. Yikes!

● Elevates the influence of states with lower populations
● Two 21st-century presidents won despite losing the popular vote
● The two presidents were George W. Bush and Donald Trump

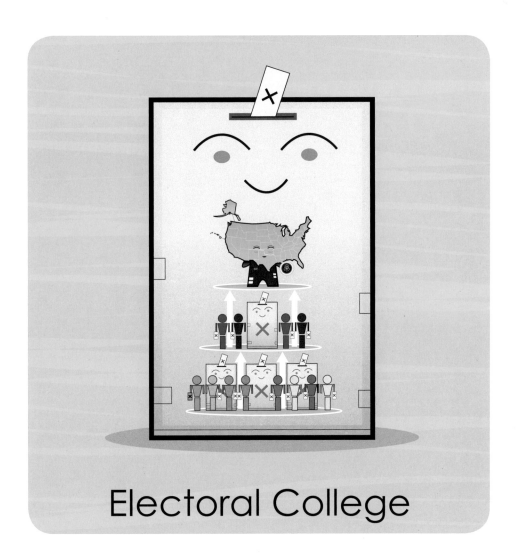

Electoral College

Chapter 2
The Law Makers

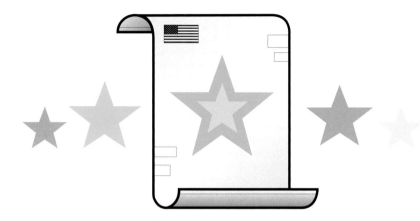

Ever wonder why you have to go to school, why you can't vote until you're 18, or why there's tax on the things you buy? It's all up to us, the Law Makers! From local city councils to state legislatures and Congress, we make the laws that impact daily life. Legislative Process determines how Bill becomes law, and the government uses Taxation to pay for things. This includes everything from the money spent on welfare programs to the roads that take you to school and the bridges you cross on the way. And all of this is in the hands of the House of Representatives and the Senate.

Congress

House of
Representatives

Senate

Bill

Legislative
Process

Taxation

Declaration
of War

Treaty

Presidential
Impeachment

Congress
The Law Makers

* The law-making branch of the U.S. government
* Made up of senators and representatives
* Elected—and can be replaced—by the voting public

I'm the star of the U.S. government's legislative branch, a collection of people who meet at the Capitol in Washington, D.C. My power was laid down in the First Article of the Constitution in 1787. I'm proud to tell you the framers of the Constitution wanted the first branch of government to be the one closest to the people.

My two "houses," the House of Representatives and the Senate, debate which ideas should become law. They also have the power to confirm judges and other officials appointed by the president. They aim to maintain a balance in the law-making process. Ideas are discussed in each house in turn until they are either agreed on or rejected. If most members agree on a law, they send it to the president, who has 10 days to sign or veto it.

* A record-breaking 127 women served in the 116th Congress (2019–21)
* Youngest woman elected to Congress: Alexandria Ocasio-Cortez, 2018 (age 29)
* The Cherokee Nation sent its first delegate to Congress in 2019

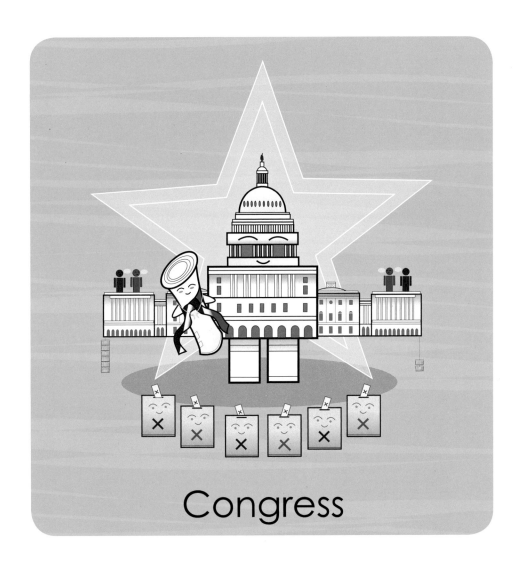

Congress

House of Representatives

The Law Makers

✳ Represents people in the districts of America's 50 states
✳ Each member represents around 750,000 people
✳ Has the power of impeachment; the Senate holds the trial

You can call me "the House," if you like. I make up one half of Congress and my 435 members are called representatives. They are divided between America's 50 states, and each representative serves a district of voters for a term of two years. States with bigger populations have more representatives.

My leader is known as the Speaker of the House. He or she is elected by whichever political party has the majority. The speaker sets the daily calendar. Speakers also get to decide which representatives sit on each committee (a smaller group focusing on certain policy issues), and act as the moderator during debates.

● The House passes legislation by a simple majority vote
● First black House representative: Joseph H. Rainey, 1870
● First female Speaker of the House: Nancy Pelosi, 2007

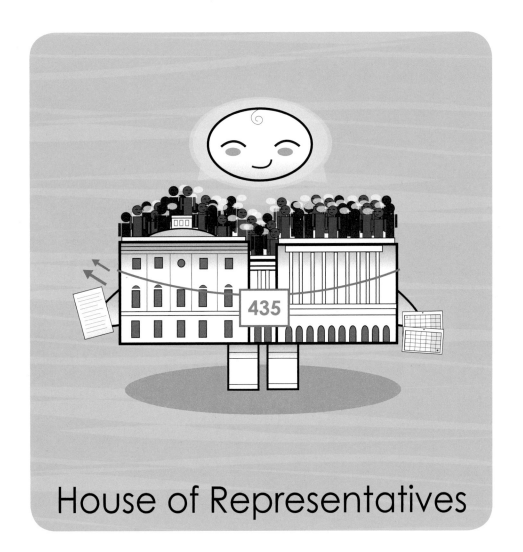

House of Representatives

Senate
■ The Law Makers

✳ Represents the people in America's 50 states
✳ The vice president is the president of the Senate
✳ Members address each other as "Senator," not by name

I am sometimes called the "upper" house of Congress. That's because my members, or senators, serve longer terms—six years instead of representatives' two. There are two senators for every U.S. state, which means each state is represented equally, no matter how high its population.

My members approve the cabinet members of the executive branch and all federal judges of the judicial branch, including Supreme Court justices. They ratify (make valid) treaties and act as the jury in cases of impeachment. The dominant political party elects a Majority Leader to create an agenda and to schedule times for debating and voting. The vice president gets to vote if there's a tie. Our title might come from the Latin word for "old man" (*senex*), but more and more women are joining our ranks!

● Minimum age to be a senator: 30 years old
● Oldest person to serve as a senator: Strom Thurmond, 100 on retirement in 2003
● First Native American senator: Charles Curtis, 1907

Senate

Bill

The Law Makers

* A proposal introduced in Congress to become law
* As many as 15,000 bills are proposed each year
* Once passed, a bill becomes a statute (law)

I'm a ray of hope, an idea that often starts off small and takes shape gradually in the two houses of Congress. Sometimes I come from Congress itself, and other times I come from people contacting Congress. Either way, thousands of my kind come into being each year, with the luckiest of us getting passed into law.

My goal is to introduce legislation to improve an aspect of society—education, health care, civil rights, taxation, the environment, you name it. I start to take shape when a member of either house in Congress formally presents me to colleagues. Once that has happened, I embark on my long journey toward becoming an actual law, or statute (I hope). Turn the page and my friend Legislative Process will tell you all about it.

● House bills and Senate bills are abbreviated to H.B. and S.B. respectively
● Students wrote the Civil Rights Cold Case Records Collection Act of 2018
● If a committee "tables" a bill, it is unlikely to be discussed again

Bill

Legislative Process
■ The Law Makers

* ✹ The process that turns a bill into a statute (law)
* ✹ All bills pass through both houses in Congress
* ✹ Each bill undergoes many rounds of tweaking

I take my friend Bill on the long journey that sees it grow from an initial idea into a proposal good enough to be passed as law. There are many twists and turns along the way, and hopeful Bill is not always successful.

Once a Congress member in either house "sponsors" (or introduces) a bill, it goes before a committee. If the committee shows enough support for the bill, the whole house debates it and votes on whether or not it should become law. Each bill must be passed by both houses in the same form. If the majority of house members vote for the bill, it goes to the president, who has 10 days to sign it. Of course, the president can choose to veto the bill. That's another story altogether. My friend Veto will tell you all about it in Chapter 3.

* ● When House members vote, they call out "yes" or "no"
* ● Both houses can "override" presidential vetoes with a two-thirds vote
* ● Some laws expire and need to be "reauthorized" (passed again)

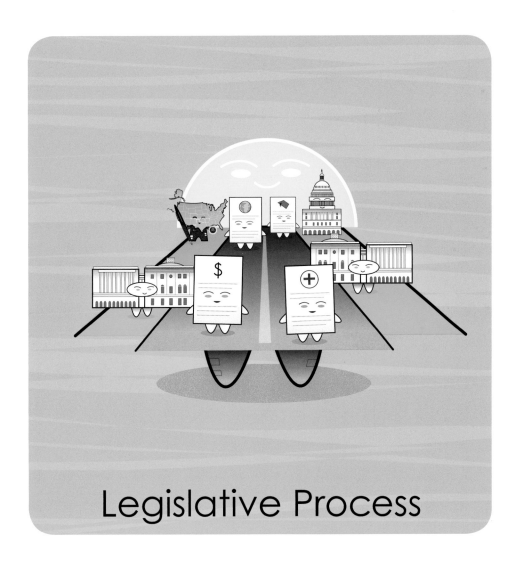

Legislative Process

Taxation
■ The Law Makers

✳ Provides a common fund to pay for government services
✳ Different types of taxes pay for specific things
✳ Federal taxes are collected by the Internal Revenue Service

Have you ever wondered where the money comes from to build your city's roads, or to purchase the books at the library, or to pay for the fire trucks racing to an emergency? These things are all down to me. I'm the process through which people pay money toward the government services that make society run smoothly. The government would grind to a halt without me.

There are different types of taxes. Sales tax is added to most things you buy and helps pay for local and state services such as roads and public schools. Income tax is taken out of people's paychecks and helps fund all kinds of programs, including those that protect people when they're too old to work. Property taxes help fund local schools and jobs in cities and towns.

● "Tax" comes from the Latin word *taxare*, meaning "to estimate"
● First income tax: 1862, to raise money for the Civil War
● Delaware, New Hampshire, and Oregon have no sales tax

Taxation

Declaration of War

✴ The Constitution gives Congress the power to declare war
✴ Congress also has control over the budget for warfare
✴ As commander-in-chief, the president can send in troops

According to the Constitution, only Congress has the right to use me. I have been made eleven times, from the War of 1812 to World War II. Since that last global conflict, Congress has passed authorizations of military force, while the president has taken a bigger role in deciding when to send in the troops. Congress still holds sway in military engagements, however, due to its control over the budget—conflict is costly!

Not everybody agrees with the executive branch (the president) interfering with legislative branch business. Since Congress is officially charged with declaring war, some ask, why should it be up to the president to decide when to send in the troops? One certainty is that I'm a decision that should never be made lightly.

● The Civil War was America's bloodiest, killing over 620,000 people
● Six WWII declarations of war were made, the first against Japan (1941)
● Over 2.2 million men were drafted during the Vietnam War (1955–75)

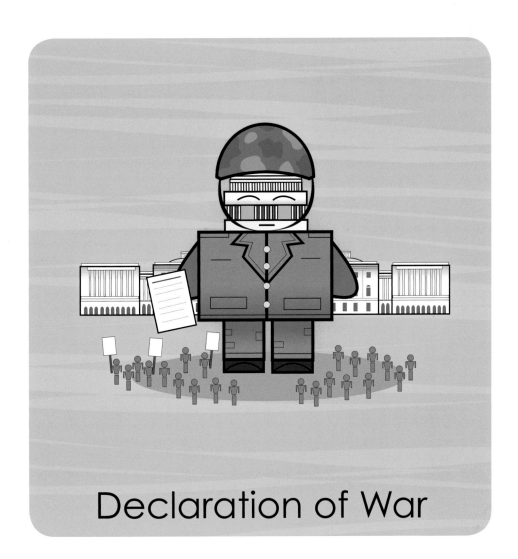

Declaration of War

Treaty
■ The Law Makers

✳ An agreement between two or more countries
✳ Must be approved by two-thirds of the Senate
✳ An important tool for diplomacy

A legal agreement between countries, I'm often used to avoid conflict and end wars. For example, the Treaty of Versailles ended World War I. In the U.S., the president has the power to make me, but not without the Senate's backing. Senators can even amend me before giving consent, or they might decide not to vote on me at all, in which case I might be withdrawn.

I have also been used as an agreement between the U.S. government and American Indian tribes. In 1830, Congress passed the Indian Removal Act. President Andrew Jackson used it to force American Indians to move from their settlements in the eastern United States to less desirable land in the west. Many treaties promising security and peace to the tribes were violated by the U.S. government.

- Oldest known treaty: Treaty of Mesilim in Mesopotamia, c. 2550 BCE
- Treaty of Paris (1783) ended the American Revolution, establishing the U.S.
- Two-party treaties are called "bilateral"; multiparty treaties are "multilateral"

Treaty

Presidential Impeachment

■ The Law Makers

☀ Holds a president accountable for their actions
☀ Each house in Congress plays a distinct role
☀ This rare process is vital for preserving democracy

Having lived under a corrupt king, the Founding Fathers wanted to be sure the United States would succeed as a democracy. That's why they included me in the Constitution—to safeguard against a president committing "Treason, Bribery, or other high Crimes and Misdemeanors."

The process starts in the House of Representatives, which makes a formal charge against the president. If the majority of representatives agrees with the charge, the Senate holds a trial. The Chief Justice of the Supreme Court presides over the trial and the Senators act like jurors. So far no president has been removed through such a trial, but I am still here, watching and waiting!

● Two-thirds of Senate members present must agree to remove the president
● In 1974, Richard Nixon faced being impeached but resigned instead
● Presidents can face civil and criminal charges after leaving office

Presidential
Impeachment

Chapter 3
The Decision Makers

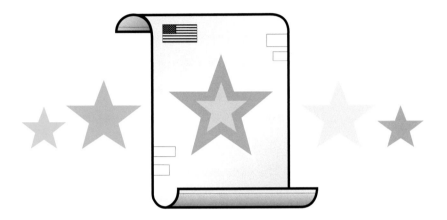

A group of movers and shakers, we're the Decision Makers! Fronted by the President, Vice President, and First Lady, we pursue goals that profoundly impact your community. See what Domestic Policy and Executive Order have to say about the influences they have over life in the 50 states. And if you want to know about relations with the rest of the world, shout out to Foreign Policy! Collectively we make up the executive branch of government. We're mighty, but as you've heard from the Constitutional Crew, even we have our limits.

President

Vice President

First Lady

The Cabinet

Governor

Veto Power

Executive
Order

Domestic
Policy

Foreign
Policy

President
■ The Decision Makers

✳ Leads the country as top member of the executive branch
✳ Serves for four years and can be re-elected for another four
✳ Presidential powers are limited by the Constitution

As head of The Decision Makers (aka the executive branch), I'm also the leader of the whole country. I'm a pretty big deal! I live in the White House, where I sign legislation passed by Congress. My pal Executive Order helps me tell the federal government what to do. And if I don't like a bill, I can use Veto Power to stop it from becoming law. I lead the country's military and team up with Foreign Policy to get along with other countries.

Even though I'm top dog, the Constitution says I have to abide by Checks and Balances. Remember those guys, and how the legislative and judicial branches have just as much power as the executive branch does? Well, if Congress finds I've abused my power, it can impeach me and kick me right out of my oval office.

● Presidents must be U.S. citizens and at least 35 years of age
● Youngest president ever elected: John F. Kennedy, at age 43
● Barack Obama made history as America's first black President in 2008

President

Vice President
■ The Decision Makers

✳ No. 2 in the executive branch hierarchy
✳ Has limited power, but steps in when needed
✳ A political speechmaker and globe-trotter

Beep, beep. Make way for the Veep! The second-highest member of the executive branch, I cast the deciding vote in the Senate if there's a 50–50 tie. Plus, I get to take over if the president can't do their job anymore. I might "only" be the VP, but I still get my share of the spotlight: I travel far and wide to speak at events and meet with world leaders. Watch me shine!

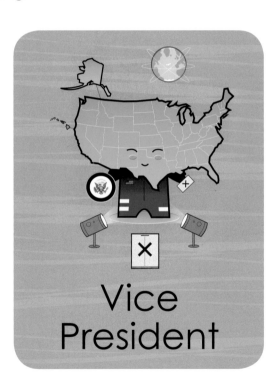

Vice President

- John Adams was the first vice president
- Number of VPs who have gone on to be president: 14
- The VP lives in a house on the grounds of the U.S. Naval Observatory

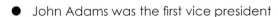

First Lady

The Decision Makers

* ✳ The title given to the president's wife
* ✳ Helps raise public awareness of important social issues
* ✳ Has an office in the East Wing of the White House

First Lady

Don't underestimate me! I'm so much more than a White House hostess. I play an active role in changing the lives of others. Eleanor Roosevelt, the longest-serving first lady, championed the rights of women and African Americans. While every person married to a president has been a woman, I just know there'll be a First Gentleman in the years to come!

- The press called George Washington's wife Martha "Lady Washington"
- Dolley Madison was the first to be called "first lady" (1809)
- Former first lady Hillary Clinton ran for president herself, in 2016

The Cabinet
■ The Decision Makers

✳ A team of top advisors to the president
✳ Experts on important issues and crucial to government
✳ Members change with each new president

Where would the president be without us? A team of trusted advisors, we direct the 15 departments that make up the government's executive branch. Just think of us as the mechanics who keep the whole presidential machine running.

The president chooses each head of department and, if the Senate approves, those people form the Cabinet. Each department takes care of an issue affecting American citizens. For example, the Department of Health and Human Services is in charge of health care, ensuring drugs are safe and effective, and stopping the spread of diseases. The Department of State focuses on the United States' relationships with other countries. Yup, we're an important bunch and the president is lucky to have us!

● "Cabinet" comes from the Italian *cabinetto*, meaning "small, private room"
● There are no rules as to how big the cabinet should be
● First cabinet: Attorney General; secretaries of the Treasury, of State, and of War

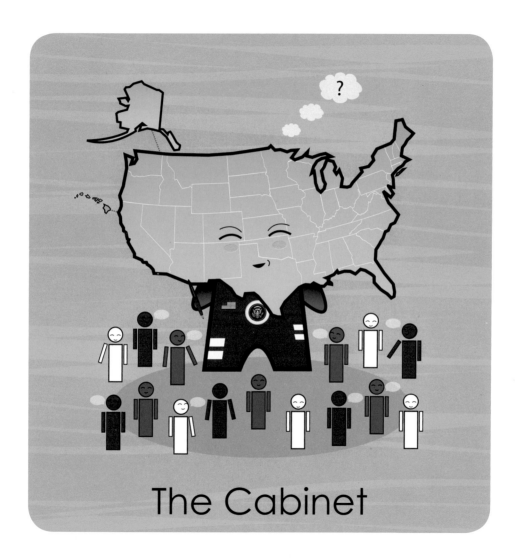

The Cabinet

Governor
■ The Decision Makers

✳ The elected head of a U.S. state or territory
✳ Takes action on state-specific initiatives and policies
✳ Often found residing in a Governor's Mansion

My job is like that of the president, only I run one state or territory instead of the whole country. Phew! Each of the 50 U.S. states has its own governor, as do the territories of American Samoa, Guam, the Northern Mariana Islands, Puerto Rico, and the U.S. Virgin Islands.

My job takes skill! I have to balance federal laws with the needs of my people, while implementing legislation passed by my own state's lawmakers. I also work with my state courts to see justice is done. Like the president, I can team up with Veto Power and Executive Order to get my way. They'll tell you how it all works. Besides all that, you'll find me managing state budgets, proposing great new lawmaking ideas, and hosting very important state guests at my mansion. It's a juggling act, for sure!

● First female U.S. governor: Nellie Tayloe Ross of Wyoming, 1924
● Lieutenant governors serve under governors—all but five states have one
● Sam Houston (1793–1863) was the only person to be governor of two states

Governor

Veto Power
The Decision Makers

* Stated in Article 1, Section 7 of the Constitution
* The presidential power to stop legislation from becoming law
* Can be overruled if two-thirds of Congress disagree

The president has special powers, one of which is to veto legislation passed by Congress. *Veto* is Latin for "I forbid." If a president strongly disagrees with legislation and doesn't think it should become law, I step in to strike that bill down like a mighty bolt of lightning! Take care though, President, as Congress can override me, after which the legislation becomes law.

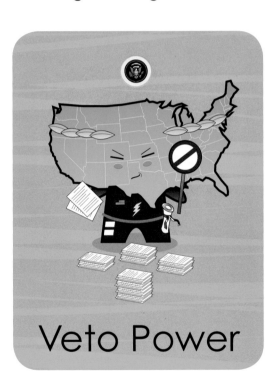

Veto Power

- President who issued the most vetoes (635): Franklin D. Roosevelt
- Number of presidents who never vetoed a bill: 7
- President James Garfield named his dog Veto

Executive Order
The Decision Makers

* Stated in Article 2 of the Constitution
* Allows the president to shape federal policy
* Not always successful—a court can strike it down

Executive Order

Aren't *I* official looking! I work with the president to direct how the federal government should operate. For example, I might insist upon establishing a policy that Congress is trying to block. I'm not always popular (surprise, surprise), and can make Congress and the voters mad. Courts sometimes need to review me to make sure I'm following the law.

* Abraham Lincoln used an early form of executive order to end slavery
* An executive order forced Japanese Americans into internment camps in WWII
* Dwight D. Eisenhower used one to help desegregate Arkansas schools

57

Domestic Policy
■ The Decision Makers

✹ Government programs relating to Americans' daily lives
✹ Influenced by the president and carried out by Congress
✹ Paid for through the congressional budget

Let's get down to business! I'm responsible for laws that have an impact on people living in America. I look at the schools you go to. I see what health care is available. I think about taxation, pollution, and discrimination.

When running for president, candidates create domestic policy platforms. They outline what they believe in and list the actions they would take to make their policies happen. Once in office, the president makes a yearly "State of the Union" speech about the living standards of U.S. citizens, and discusses ways to improve them. You'll hear the president mention the "economy." This relates to the money-based resources the country has. These resources are vital to improving living standards. It's my job to create policies that keep the economy strong.

● The New Deal (1933–36) helped America recover from the Great Depression
● One major public policy Americans debate today is gun control
● Almost all Western countries except America have universal health care

Domestic Policy

Foreign Policy
■ The Decision Makers

✴ Concerns relationships with countries outside the United States
✴ Influences how the world perceives America
✴ Presidents have wide power to shape and command

Let's change the world! When it comes to working with countries outside the United States, I'm the one in charge. I shape the ways in which U.S. government departments, businesses, and organizations interact with the rest of the world. I help countries in trouble by giving them aid, I address human rights issues, and I work with others to promote peace. I even handle Congress's declarations of war! Sure, the president sets the policy goals for what I do, but I'm the one who does all the work.

It is important that I look after the "special relationships" the U.S. shares with certain countries, such as the United Kingdom and Canada. Being on best-buddy terms can help when it comes to trading goods, organizing military operations abroad, or sharing top-secret intelligence.

● Prioritizes the protection of America and its allies
● Supports the idea of democracy around the world
● Seeks to protect the global balance of power

Foreign Policy

Chapter 4
Courtroom Crowd

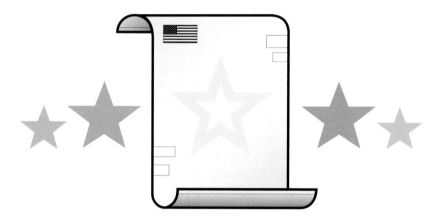

Featuring courts of all sorts, this chapter introduces the mainstays of the judicial branch: state courts, federal courts, appeals courts—you name it. Right at the top, the mighty Supreme Court has the final say on legal matters. To uphold justice, this crowd must treat everybody fairly and equally, no matter who they are, where they come from, or how much power and privilege they hold in society. Here's your chance to find out more. Learn the difference between Criminal Case and Civil Case and acquaint yourself with Trial by Jury and Precedent.

Courts

Supreme Court

Trial by Jury

Civil Case

Criminal Case

Precedent

Courts
Courtroom Crowd

✳ Courts hear cases between two or more opposing parties
✳ State, district, and federal courts have different jurisdictions
✳ Multiple levels lead up to the highest: the Supreme Court

Decisions! Decisions! That's what we make. We form the backbone of the judicial branch. We administer justice fairly, and act as the remedy when people, companies, organizations, and even the government break the law. Without us, lawbreakers wouldn't be punished and disputes between people couldn't be settled.

Each state has a court system, including a supreme court (but don't confuse this with the U.S. Supreme Court on the next page!). State courts deal with legal disputes within a city or state. Federal courts oversee lawsuits against the U.S. government and cases about federal law. The U.S. Supreme Court considers disputes between two or more states. If you don't like our decisions, you can appeal, but you need a strong case!

● Civil courts hear disputes between people
● In criminal courts, the state brings cases against suspected lawbreakers
● Appellate courts are the "last stop" before the Supreme Court

Courts

Supreme Court
Courtroom Crowd

✴ The country's highest court
✴ Has the power to undo the decisions of lower courts
✴ Interprets the Constitution as it applies to modern life

I'm the top dog of the judicial system. What I say goes. These days, I have nine justices at my disposal—three of them are women. Nominated by the president and confirmed by the Senate, once my justices are appointed, they get to stay with me for the rest of their lives. (Oliver Wendell Holmes was 90 when he retired!)

Using a power called judicial review, I get to determine whether laws passed by Congress are in line with the Constitution. Sometimes, I've made decisions that expand liberty, but some of my rulings have also caused great harm. In 1857, I ruled that Dred Scott should stay enslaved because black people didn't count as citizens. My Law Maker pal Amendment put this right in the 1860s, abolishing slavery and granting citizenship to black Americans.

● The "lead" justice is called the Chief Justice
● First female Supreme Court justice: Sandra Day O'Connor, 1981
● First woman of color on the Supreme Court: Sonia Sotomayor, 2009

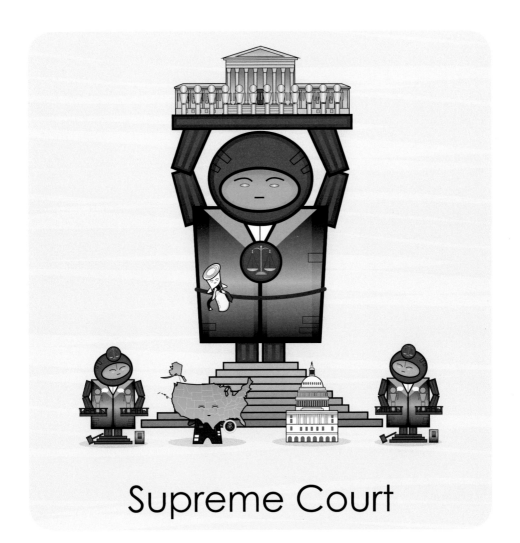

Supreme Court

Trial by Jury
Courtroom Crowd

* The right to a fair, unbiased trial
* Guaranteed by the 6th and 7th Amendments
* Juries allow U.S. citizens to participate in the courts

Key to democracy, I allow a person accused of a crime to have their case heard by a "jury of peers." My Good Citizen pal Jury Duty will tell you how it works. Lawyers present evidence to the jury in front of a judge, who asks the jury members to focus purely on the facts of the case and not on any preconceived notions of their own.

Once all the evidence has been heard, the jurors (jury members) vote on a defendant's guilt or innocence and give their decision, known as the "verdict." The judge then decides the punishment, if any. Criminal cases have 12 jurors, though civil cases can have fewer. In most states, all jurors must agree on the verdict. If they don't, the result is a "hung jury." If this happens, a new trial often presents all the evidence again, but with different jurors.

● "Juror" comes from the French *jurer*, "to swear [an oath]"
● U.S. citizens are required to serve on juries when asked
● The size of jury varies from state to state and depends on the type of case

Trial by Jury

Civil Case
Courtroom Crowd

☀ Private parties can sue each other for civil wrongdoing
☀ Individuals, groups, or corporations can all sue or be sued
☀ Decisions are based on evidence presented in court

When someone (the "plaintiff") says they've been wronged and files a civil lawsuit against another party (the "defendant,") that's where I come in. I decide who's to blame and make the wrongdoer pay! Say someone sold you a bike that didn't work, but wouldn't give your money back. You could sue the store and (if you won) I'd make sure you got your money back or a new bike!

Civil Case

● Some actions can result in both civil and criminal charges
● A group of people can file a "class-action" lawsuit together
● Most civil cases are heard by a judge rather than a jury

Criminal Case
Courtroom Crowd

* Tries serious crimes that make society less safe
* To convict, evidence must be "beyond a reasonable doubt"
* The 4th–8th Amendments provide rights to those accused

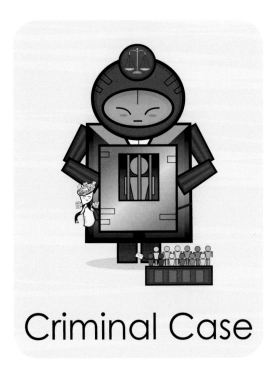

Criminal Case

I'm here to punish crimes that harm society, such as theft, drunk driving, and even murder. For example, if someone stole that bike you just bought, the state would bring the case on your behalf. A jury has to decide "beyond reasonable doubt" whether the defendant(s) are guilty or not. Serious crimes result in a jail sentence, or even the death penalty.

● Oldest known law code: Ur-Nammu in Mesopotamia, 2100–2050 BCE
● The 6th Amendment guarantees a criminal defendant's right to an attorney
● Today, 20 states have abolished the death penalty

Precedent
Courtroom Crowd

✴ A past court judgment cited as an example in a new case
✴ Used to justify arriving at a similar judgment
✴ Almost all judicial decisions are based on precedent

I'm called upon when the decision of a lower court is appealed to a higher court, such as the U.S. Supreme Court. The way the Supreme Court rules sets an example, or is used as a guide, for the lower courts to follow when deciding similar cases. I can be a big time saver!

Supreme Court decisions have resulted in some famous precedents. In Brown v. Board of Education of Topeka (1954), for example, the court ruled that school segregation—forcing students of color to go to different schools than white students—was unconstitutional because "separate educational facilities are inherently unequal." That ruling meant all U.S. schools had to desegregate. It also served as precedent for future segregation lawsuits.

● Binding precedent: an existing law that must be followed
● Persuasive precedent: influential in reaching a decision, but not binding
● Precedent can still be overruled by new decisions or legislation

Precedent

Chapter 5
Good Citizens

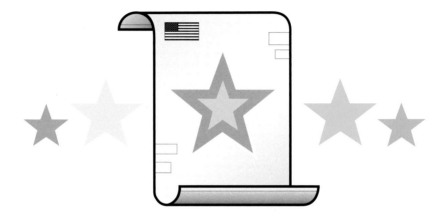

Come and say hello to the Good Citizens, a diverse crew who will tell you more about life in the United States. Citizenship and Universal Suffrage want to talk about rights, while Voting, Jury Duty, and Personal Participation are all about your responsibilities. Political Parties and Gerrymandering explain how different groups get involved in government. And Immigration points out that people from other countries can live in the U.S. too. Towering above them all, Statue of Liberty embraces those who come to the country to pursue their dreams and enjoy the freedoms of U.S. citizens.

Citizenship

Immigration

Statue of
Liberty

Universal
Suffrage

Voting

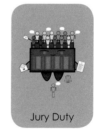

Jury Duty

Political Party

Gerrymandering

Personal
Participation

Citizenship
■ Good Citizens

* ✴ When a person is considered a full member of a country
* ✴ Anyone born in the United States has citizenship there
* ✴ Can also be gained through a process called naturalization

Born in the USA! That's me! But that's not the whole story. Just ask my pal Immigration. In the United States, citizenship includes having rights granted by the government and being protected by its laws. In return, citizens agree to be loyal to the United States, and to carry out particular "duties," the most important of which is voting.

People from other countries can also receive my benefits. To do so, they need to have lived in the United States legally for at least five years and must pledge allegiance to the country. They become a "permanent resident" and take steps toward "naturalization," which include taking a test. The whole process is expensive, complicated, and lengthy, but at the end of it all, there I am to greet them!

* ● Around 680,000 people become naturalized citizens each year
* ● More than 7.2 million people became naturalized citizens in the last decade
* ● Naturalized citizens cannot run for president or vice president

Citizenship

Immigration
■ Good Citizens

* ✹ When a person moves from one country to live in another
* ✹ People often immigrate in search of a better life
* ✹ Has produced the diverse U.S. nation we see today

I am the process through which people move from one country or territory to another, with the intention of living there permanently. Most Americans today are either immigrants themselves or descended from immigrants. I'm a big part of the story of the United States. Who do you think brought in most of the people who helped build this country?

Immigration

- ● 1st first lady born outside the United States: Louisa Catherine Johnson Adams
- ● Anti-immigrant laws (such as the Chinese Exclusion Act) have long histories
- ● Immigrants made up almost 14% of the U.S. population in 2017

Statue of Liberty
Good Citizens

* This iconic New York landmark was a gift from the French
* Represents Libertas, the Roman goddess of liberty
* Stands testimony to America's embrace of immigrants

Statue of Liberty

In 1886, to thank America for abolishing slavery and inspiring the French Revolution, France sent me as a gift. Today, I stand on Liberty Island, in New York Harbor, with a poem by Emma Lazarus at my base. Calling me the "Mother of Exiles," it has me proclaim, "'Give me your tired, your poor, / . . . Send these, the homeless, tempest-tost to me, / I lift my lamp beside the golden door!'"

* Stands 305 feet (93 m) tall
* Sculpted by Frédéric Auguste Bartholdi
* Gustave Eiffel, of Eiffel Tower fame, built the metal infrastructure

Universal Suffrage
■ Good Citizens

✳ Achieved when all citizens have the right to vote
✳ Many minority groups have had to fight for voting rights
✳ Even after rights are granted, discrimination still happens

The Declaration of Independence says that "all men are created equal," but equality has not always been the case when it comes to voting in the United States. Initially "men" literally meant *white men only*, and people of color couldn't vote at all! The right for all adult citizens to vote is called universal suffrage—that's me!

After slavery ended, black men weren't legally allowed to vote until 1870. Even then, some faced intimidation and laws to stop them voting up through 1965. This was when civil rights activists got the Voting Rights Act passed. Meanwhile, and after several decades of protest, women finally got the vote in 1920. But not all women could vote; American Indian and Asian women had to wait longer still until they were granted suffrage.

● Seneca Falls Convention, 1848: launch of U.S. women's suffrage movement
● Indian Citizenship Act, 1924: granted American Indians citizenship
● McCarran-Walter Act, 1952: gave Asian-Americans citizenship and voting rights

Universal Suffrage

Voting
■ Good Citizens

✳ Fundamental to democratic government
✳ Helps settle important issues when people don't agree
✳ Is available to U.S. citizens only

What's the point of Universal Suffrage without me? If you have been given the right to vote, be sure to use it! I am one way in which you can have your say in the things that matter to you most. I allow you to back political issues and candidates that you believe in. So come on, get out there and make yourself heard!

OK, so you have to be 18 years old before you can vote, but that day will come. When it does, you simply register in your home state. You'll probably do it online, after which you'll be able to vote in most local, state, and federal elections. Of course, I like my system to be fair. Sometimes Gerrymandering creeps in, or foreign governments interfere in elections. These things can reflect badly on me and my reputation suffers.

● The voting age in the U.S. was 21 until 1971
● 58% of registered voters voted in the presidential election of 2016
● Residents of U.S. territories cannot vote in a presidential election

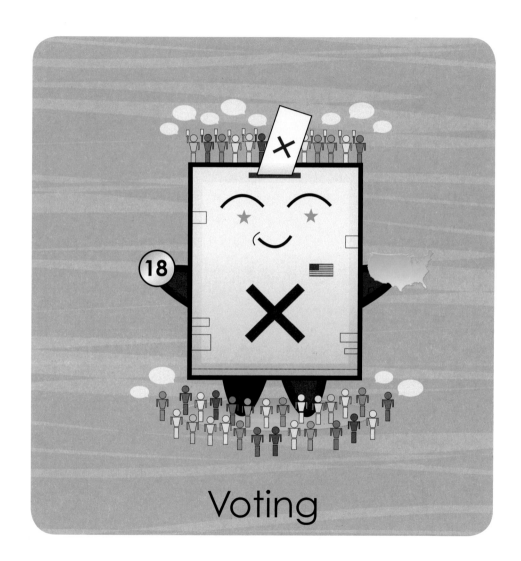

Voting

Jury Duty
Good Citizens

* A process that sees citizens play a role in the judicial system
* In some trials, jurors decide a defendant's guilt or innocence
* In criminal trials, a jury is made up of 12 jurors

Remember my Courtroom Crowd pal, Trial by Jury? I'm the process that brings members of the community into the courtroom in the first place. I'm one of those "duties" that Citizenship talked about several pages back—something required of all adult U.S. citizens.

You need to have a good reason for turning down my invitation to serve. You see, I'm a crucial link in the democratic processes that underpin life in the United States. It's my service that reassures a defendant that their trial is going to be fair, and I think that's pretty important. I can last anything from a couple of days to several weeks, or even months. People may grumble about the time they lose at work or with their families, but I say it's worth it to see that justice has been done.

● Potential jurors are picked randomly from voting and driving records
● People convicted of felony crimes (imprisonable offences) can't be jurors
● Jurors receive a small payment for their participation

Jury Duty

Political Party

✳ There are two main political parties in the United States
✳ The Democratic Party is thought to be more liberal
✳ The Republican Party is thought to be more conservative

When people vote for candidates for most offices, they are voting for one of my members. I'm Political Party, an organized group of people who want the same things when it comes to politics.

I take many forms. For example, smaller parties exist in the United States (say, the Greens and the Libertarians). Such groups bring attention to important ideas that are sometimes adopted by one of the major parties. The Green Party, for example, is very committed to environmental justice. But most elections are won by the Democrats or the Republicans. Some say this "two-party" system limits voters' options. Maybe that's why more Americans currently identify as "independents" rather than as either Democrats or Republicans.

● First U.S. political parties: the Federalists and the Democratic-Republicans
● First Democratic president: Andrew Jackson, 7th U.S. president
● First Republican president: Abraham Lincoln, 16th U.S. president

Political Party

Gerrymandering

✳ Moving district boundaries to sway the outcome of an election
✳ Named for Massachusetts governor Elbridge Gerry (1744–1814)
✳ Both Democrats and Republicans participate in this practice

"Cracking" and "packing" my way across a state, I'm a sneaky type who shifts the boundaries of a district to take advantage of the way people vote. I plot with Political Party to secure seats in the House of Representatives.

All districts have roughly the same number of inhabitants, so how do I operate? Well, I can "pack" the opposition's voters into just one or two of a state's districts to allow a majority there, but nowhere else. Or I can "crack" a district open, making boundaries that leave voters spread out across many districts. This way one party gains no majority at all! I have a bad rep. More than 200 years ago I made a district in the shape of a salamander and the "mander" part of my name has been a reminder of that lizard-like creature ever since. But what do I care?

● Congressional boundaries are redrawn every ten years
● Districts should reflect the distribution of voters between the parties
● Suspected cases of gerrymandering may end up in court

Gerrymandering

Personal Participation
■ Good Citizens

☀ Kids can help change society
☀ It takes critical thinking, active listening, caring, taking action
☀ Any difference you make now will only be the beginning

There are ways in which you—yes, you, reading this right now—can participate in government. The first step is to learn about issues impacting your family and community. Listen to people you've never talked to before. Collect their stories and gather evidence from reliable sources, such as books, newspapers, and other media. Ask questions. For example, are people in your community in need of basic resources such as food, housing, and health care? Do your elected officials do a good job of finding solutions? Can you think of ways to make life better?

If you have a great idea, become an activist. Write to your elected officials, or post on social media. Help out with a food drive, volunteer at a pet adoption day, or organize a student protest. You can make a difference!

● Malala Yousafzai was just 11 when she started her girls' education campaign
● Swedish climate justice activist Greta Thunberg started protesting at 15
● Florida teens organized the 2018 March for Our Lives

Personal Participation

Bill of Rights

Amendment I Congress shall make no law respecting an establishment of religion, or prohibiting the free exercise thereof; or abridging the freedom of speech, or of the press; or the right of the people peaceably to assemble, and to petition the Government for a redress of grievances.

Amendment II A well regulated Militia, being necessary to the security of a free State, the right of the people to keep and bear Arms, shall not be infringed.

Amendment III No Soldier shall, in time of peace be quartered in any house, without the consent of the Owner, nor in time of war, but in a manner to be prescribed by law.

Amendment IV The right of the people to be secure in their persons, houses, papers, and effects, against unreasonable searches and seizures, shall not be violated, and no Warrants shall issue, but upon probable cause, supported by Oath or affirmation, and particularly describing the place to be searched, and the persons or things to be seized.

Amendment V No person shall be held to answer for a capital, or otherwise infamous crime, unless on a presentment or indictment of a Grand Jury, except in cases arising in the land or naval forces, or in the Militia, when in actual service in time of War or public danger; nor shall any person be subject for the same offence to be twice put in jeopardy of life or limb; nor shall be compelled in any criminal case to be a witness against himself, nor be deprived of life, liberty, or property, without due process of law; nor shall private property be taken for public use, without just compensation.

Amendment VI In all criminal prosecutions, the accused shall enjoy the right to a speedy and public trial, by an impartial jury of the State and district wherein the crime shall have been committed, which district shall have been previously ascertained by law, and to be informed of the nature and cause of the accusation; to be confronted with the witnesses against him; to have compulsory process for obtaining witnesses in his favor, and to have the Assistance of Counsel for his defense.

Amendment VII In suits at common law, where the value in controversy shall exceed twenty dollars, the right of trial by jury shall be preserved, and no fact tried by a jury, shall be otherwise reexamined in any Court of the United States, than according to the rules of the common law.

Amendment VIII Excessive bail shall not be required, nor excessive fines imposed, nor cruel and unusual punishments inflicted.

Amendment IX The enumeration in the Constitution, of certain rights, shall not be construed to deny or disparage others retained by the people.

Amendment X The powers not delegated to the United States by the Constitution, nor prohibited by it to the States, are reserved to the States respectively, or to the people.

Glossary

Activist: Someone who believes in a cause and takes bold action to create change in society.

Appeal: When someone loses a lawsuit and seeks a new opinion from a higher court; the U.S. Supreme Court has the final say.

Budget: The way a person or group decides to spend their money, including which expenses are prioritized.

Civics: The study of government and ways that citizens participate in government to make society better.

Civil rights: The right to be treated equally under the law regardless of race, gender, disability, and many other factors; fought for by activists.

Civil War: U.S. war (1861–65) between the North and South over enslavement; the North won and slavery was abolished.

Conservative: Political beliefs that usually emphasize "traditional" values and resist social change; they tend to favor free enterprise and private ownership.

Desegregation: The act of removing the restrictions that barred people of color from the same schools, businesses, and neighborhoods as white people.

Diplomacy: The act of building and maintaining positive relationships between different countries' governments to ensure peace.

Discrimination: When a group with power in society mistreats another group and prevents it from having equal resources, opportunities, or rights.

District (congressional): A certain area of land (decided by state legislatures or independent commissions) from which voters elect a member of the House of Representatives.

Economy: The system in which money is made and spent in a country, including how much money families make and how the government spends tax money.

Federal: A political system in which a number of states agree to be governed by one central authority.

Feminism: The belief that people are equal regardless of gender; it began as a women's political movement in the 19th century and continues today.

Liberal: Political beliefs that usually emphasize equality, civil rights, and government spending to help vulnerable groups.

Monarch: A king or queen; a country where a king or queen rules or has a formal position is called a monarchy.

Naturalization: The complex legal process through which an immigrant becomes a U.S. citizen.

Independents: Voters who decline to call themselves Democrats or Republicans;

their votes can influence election results even though they are not members of a formal political party.

Privilege: The set of unearned advantages and preferential treatment a person may have in society due to their race, gender, or other characteristics.

Protest: The act of standing up against powerful people, laws, or governments that are considered unjust, in support of a cause.

Slavery (transatlantic): Europeans' transport of millions of Africans to the Americas, forcing them to work for no pay and to become the property of their enslavers (15th–19th centuries).

Territories (U.S.): Land colonized by the U.S. government and which the U.S. still controls even while granting some autonomy (but not statehood).

Welfare program: Policies enacted by the government to help struggling families, such as by providing health care and money for food.

Index